ROB2

Paintings, Sketches, and Reminiscences
of a Vanishing World

ARCTIC JOURNEY

by Peter Buerschaper

PAGURIAN PRESS LIMITED
TORONTO

ISBN 0-88932-059-4
Printed and bound in Canada

TO
BEV

Contents

Foreword

To find the physical ruggedness and endurance needed to cope with the harshness of the high arctic environment and an artistic awareness in one person is rare. These qualities are ideally combined in Peter Buerschaper. Add a passion for the north country, a background of scientific discipline, and the ability to render his impressions in colour and in black and white, and he emerges as a very uncommon person indeed; and a much needed one.

Certain aspects of Canada's high arctic archipelago have been largely overlooked by artists. It is true that a number of painters, some of them distinguished ones, have interpreted the land. Almost without exception (and I speak from first-hand observation of some of them in the field) they have been overwhelmed by the immensities of the landscapes where one's vision is never restrained by trees. Powerful paintings of great barren mountains, of vast ice-fields and icebergs and glaciers have been made but these things are not necessarily unique to arctic regions; rather the arctic, to the seasoned traveller and the artist-naturalist, is made up of many smaller and more intimate things,—a fragile saxifrage blooming a yard away from the ice-hard névé of a gully so sheltered from the sun that it *never* melts; a golden plover in a snowstorm; a snow bunting perched on a rib of a musk-ox skeleton perhaps a decade or more old—for decay is slow in the arctic; an inquisitive wolf, not just any wolf but a white, gangly long-legged arctic wolf; the odd shapes of eroded ice, the gay colours of living lichens, and the delicate fragrance of tiny arctic flowers—of such things is the arctic made. They are the immediate and exclusive things of the land where the struggle for the continuance of individual and species life is desperate.

Each of Peter Buerschaper's paintings brought back nostalgic memories; some exciting and reminiscent of the volatility of the arctic summer; others of the feeling of melancholy and forboding that is inescapable to the sensitive person who treads the tundra.

I know that many will join me in the hope that the all-too-brief expedition that resulted in the diary and the paintings that make up this book is but the first of many high arctic artistic adventures that will be undertaken by Peter Buerschaper.

The arctic needs his empathetic interpretations.

Terence Michael Shortt
Wildlife artist and author of
Wild Birds of Canada and the Americas

Acknowledgments

Many people generously and willingly contributed their time and effort to this project. My sincere thanks

to Stewart MacDonald who invited me to accompany him on his expedition during the spring of 1976 to the Canadian high arctic;

to the arctic travellers who lived in the Bathurst Island camp that year and made me feel so welcome;

to Terence Shortt whose constant encouragement provided me with the initiative to undertake and complete this project;

to Mrs. Cheryl Goodchild for her help in translating my poor handwriting into type and for her constructive comments on the text;

to Margaret Rowlands who donated her time to type page after page of the original manuscript;

to George Coker and Peter Lore who gave of their time when deadlines had to be met during the various stages of composition;

to the people of the Royal Ontario Museum who provided extra time for me away from my job to take part in the arctic expedition. I thank Dr. E.J. Crossman, Dr. J.E. Cruise, and Dr. A.R. Emery;

to Christopher Ondaatje for giving me the opportunity to paint and write about my arctic excursion.

Departure

The incoming Nordair flight is late. The jet was to have taken off from Resolute Bay at 11:15 P.M. At midnight there is still no sign of it. It has been explained to us that because of bad fog conditions in Frobisher Bay, the flight would be delayed for some time.

It is the third of July. The midnight sun beams through the greasy windows of the Resolute Bay airport waiting room. Outside it is calm. The sun gleams off the still snow-covered hills just north of the gravel runway. The shadows are a bit longer than during the daytime, and the overall colouring of the surrounding landscape is a bit warmer — one has to have been here for a while to be able to differentiate between day and night. With the temperature hovering around 0°C, it is hard to believe that it is July.

The waiting room is hot and crowded. For more than an hour people have been gathering to catch the southbound flight. Suitcases, sleeping bags, and an assortment of cardboard boxes are everywhere, creating an obstacle course for anyone wanting to walk around the room.

One of the Eskimos from the Resolute Bay Eskimo village has come to wish everyone a pleasant journey south. Wearing his motorcycle helmet, he makes his way through the smoke-filled room, shaking hands and kissing ladies at every opportunity. Not all of the ladies in the room seem to appreciate his kindly gesture. It is noticeable that he has just come from a party. Speaking half in an Eskimo dialect and half in English, he misses almost no one on his well-wishing tour. Indeed, several are greeted many times. Most visitors and travellers appreciate his concern and his smiling face makes the long wait more enjoyable. His wife, who always accompanies him (so I am told), sits silently on a nearby bench, observing her husband with an expression of pride clearly visible on her gentle face.

It is Saturday night in Resolute Bay, frontier town of the Seventies. Many of the well-wishers and travellers have consumed quantities of alcohol to celebrate the weekend, or the southbound flight, or whatever. A young man with long blond hair dangling out from under a red baseball cap and sprouting a healthy growth of arctic beard has, to say the least, had one or two too many. In silence he negotiates his way through the crowded hall, clutching under one arm a cardboard box neatly held together with butcher twine. He finds a comfortable corner on the waiting room floor. There he falls asleep with one elbow on his cardboard box, his fist supporting his head, oblivious to all that is going on around him. Later I learn that he has been in the arctic since early spring working on a scientific project on one of the high arctic islands.

It is common practice for people who work in arctic regions to be sent south to remingle with humanity every few months. Supposedly this is good for their morale and keeps workers happy at their jobs.

The arctic is a valuable training ground for many young biology students. And, if only a small percentage of those who spend their summers in these most northern lands come away with some understanding of the wilderness and the need to preserve it, there is a good chance that the arctic will remain the last of our frontiers for some time to come.

NORTH
POLE

MELVILLE ISLAND

BATHURST ISLAND

AXEL HEIBERG ISLAND

Eureka

ELLESMERE ISLAND

Resolute Bay

DEVON ISLAND

BAFFIN ISLAND

GREENLAND

20

100

60

30

We wait for almost two hours for Flight 703. When it arrives, it has to be unloaded. On these northern flights, first-class sections of airliners are usually converted into cargo areas. Large loading plat-forms are filled with food and other materials needed to provide northern settlements with day-to-day necessities. They are crammed into the first-class section. Just about everything has to be flown in from the south. As much as two dollars per pound is added to anything flown to Resolute Bay, and one might as well eat steak as hamburger since the freight charge remains the same. Once a year a ship calls in the harbour and delivers all the larger commodities required for the following year. This sea lift, traditionally, also un-loads Resolute Bay's yearly beer supply. It is for this reason that the beer in the local Resolute pub may taste stale during June and July before the new supply arrives.

Unloading and reloading takes another three-quarters of an hour. Finally, the midnight sun still shining, we are airborne. Flying high over the frozen sea, we head south. After a brief stop in Frobisher Bay it is on to Montreal and back to Toronto for me. I have spent three weeks in the arctic — and the country, the people, and the wildlife have left me with a jumble of images and impressions which I have yet to sort out.

Arrival

After a wild taxi ride from a local hotel (a tradition of mine when in Montreal), I reach the Montreal airport and my arctic adventure begins. I find the appropriate gate and in the waiting room I meet Stewart MacDonald. Stu is the curator of ethology (animal behaviour studies) at the Museum of Natural Sciences in Ottawa, and he has invited me to accompany him on an expedition to the eastern high arctic. He wants to further document breeding records of birds and observe other arctic animals — what better way to be introduced to the arctic than by someone who has developed a love and appreciation for it.

We board Flight 703 and the five-hour flight from Montreal to Resolute Bay (via Frobisher Bay) passes quickly. Stu and I talk at length about our favourite topic — our fascination for wild, living things. We touch on the subject of wildlife art — the reason why I have been invited to take part in this expedition. I hope to gather impressions and sketch birds and other animals during my stay in the arctic; then paint them when I return home.

Why is wildlife art so little recognized in the art world? This, I'm convinced, stems from the days when the artist-scientist illustrated a new species (before the development of the camera) to show his discovery to the world — solely for documentation. It is true that much wildlife art produced today has little to do with art and is purely a mechanical and technical craft. Even that is not all bad. Many people appreciate and collect precision hand-tooled crafts of all descriptions, from all periods of man's endeavours — why then not wildlife art?

There are, however, wildlife artists who should be accepted as artists.

Few artists have been to the eastern high arctic and few have painted the area's wildlife. George Miksch Sutton, however, has done both. In 1968 he stayed on Bathurst Island and later produced an illustrated book on the area, *High Arctic*. It contains many water-colours, all painted on Bathurst Island. He used freshly collected specimens as models, setting them in natural habitats. His earlier work published by the Carnegie Museum in 1929-1930, *The Birds of Southampton Island*, makes excellent background reading for all arctic travellers. Between 1927 and 1968 Sutton spent much of his time in various parts of the arctic, and his wildlife art comes from first-hand observation.

Another wildlife artist whose art comes from first-hand observation is Terence Michael Shortt. He was one of two artists on the *Nascopie* during her 1938 voyage. By 1938 the *Nascopie* had already had several years' experience bumping her way through the ice floes to supply goods to the outposts of this northland. On her voyages biologists, artists, doctors, and newsmen went along to share in her adventures.

On this trip Terry produced beautiful paintings. Perhaps more than anyone, he captures the colours of the arctic in his watercolours of arctic birds. His superb pen and ink drawings, published in L. Snyder's book, *Arctic Birds of Canada* (1957), are a result of Terry's excursions. Today Terry still paints birds with a grasp of mood, colour, and behavioural and anatomical knowledge which can be acquired only from personal observation. (The other artist on the *Nascopie's* 1938 voyage was Fred Horsman Varley, of the Group of Seven fame.)

We arrive at Resolute Bay at approximately 5 P.M. The temperature is -2°C — a change from the 30°C heat wave I left behind in Toronto

Snow bunting ▶

BUERSCHAPER '76

and Montreal. Storekeepers in Toronto thought the heat had affected my brain when I bought my equipment for this expedition. Why would anyone buy woolen socks, long quilted underwear, scarves, and eiderdown-filled mittens during a mid-June southern Ontario heatwave?

I knew what I was doing because most of Resolute Bay is still blanketed by several inches of snow. Dense patches of fog obscure the hilltops.

Our gear is unloaded and taxied to living quarters at the Polar Continental Shelf Project. We are billeted in a makeshift room, slated to be an office. It is in a newly constructed, unfinished building. All other living quarters are filled with people who have arrived on our flight and are waiting to be flown to their working areas. Some researchers are destined for Somerset and Devon Islands; others are to be taken as far north as Ellesmere Island. Frequently visitors are forced to stay in Resolute Bay for days on end. Severe weather conditions, usually dense fog, leave people stranded.

Resolute Bay resembles a disarranged shipyard. Piles of equipment both new and old lie scattered around. The muddy roads just outside town are lined with lengths of pipe; hundreds of oil drums and heaps of building materials are everywhere. The mess, combined with the wet and cold climate, is a dismal introduction to the arctic. It is with distaste that one realizes that the white man's version of civilization has penetrated this far north and has made its ugly mark even here.

The fog drifts in and out but an occasional hint of sunshine burns through the fog cover from time to time. We are optimistic and hope to reach Bathurst Island tonight.

Three people are already there. David Gill, of the National Museum of Canada, is working on lemming population studies and a dozen or

◀ *Purple sandpiper*

so other projects; Jan Rowell is there to tabulate information on musk ox behaviour; and Michael McNall is continuing his behavioural studies on jaegers. All are under Stu's supervision. These three have been in the Bathurst camp since early spring (when temperatures often dip into the -30°C range).

The weather continues to improve.

A single-engine Otter airplane is loaded with gear. The smallish, cone-shaped cabin area of this vintage aircraft is crammed with our personal belongings, full forty-five-gallon oil drums, and, of all things, a frozen head of a musk ox. The head has been severed from its body to provide Stu with additional research material and is to be examined at the Bathurst Island laboratory.

We are four arctic travellers bound for Bathurst Island — John Geale and James Campbell have flown up with us from Montreal to work on Bathurst Island for the summer.

Our plane has seen better days. Mechanically it may be sound, but the wear and tear on its interior decor has taken its toll. Doors are hard to open and even harder to close. The tiny seats have seen many hours of use. Walls, floors, and ceilings are scratched.

The first single Otter airplane for use in the arctic was bought from de Havilland in 1952. Perhaps this was the one. A "one ton truck," the single Otter is the workhorse of the eastern arctic. It flies on skiis or soft balloon tires to every nook and cranny, delivering people, supplies, and mail to areas previously accessible only by dog sled. Fuel caches are stashed wherever needed, and Otters refuel in the most unlikely places.

We barrel down the runway, become airborne, and we are off. At least so we think. Half an hour later fog engulfs us. Ice collects on windshield, wings, and body. The additional weight keeps us at a low altitude. The chance of running into one of the higher ridges just ahead becomes of great concern to Mel, the pilot, and he decides to return to Resolute Bay.

At Resolute I am introduced to the local cookhouse, the meeting place of all arctic travellers. Discussion of work plans for the summer and stories of previous adventures are the main topics of conversation. Students and seasoned scientists alike gather here to exchange ideas and prepare for the expeditions ahead.

After dinner, with little else to do, we stroll through what I hesitate to call the downtown section. Brilliant orange and grass-green wooden row houses line a dirt road that opens a quarter of a mile later into the vast landscape of the arctic. Souvenirs, hand-crafted by local Eskimos, and hot showers are for sale here.

At the end of the main street there is nothing but barren ground, for the most part still covered with snow. The expanse is occasionally broken by a tiny recently formed creeklet gathering melt water.

Snow buntings

In places snow has melted exposing the gravelly ground. Here, last season's cotton grass sways in the steady wind. Mosses and lichens, revitalized by the melting snow, paint abstractions in form and colour on exposed rocks. In the distance, the call of a male snow bunting. Snowbirds (as snow buntings are called here) fly back and forth landing on rocks or patches of exposed ground.

Usually at this time of year most of the snow has melted, and the snow bunting should be sitting on a full clutch of eggs. This year, however, the breeding population on Cornwallis Island is still staking out territories, and some birds have only just begun gathering dried grasses, moss, and stray feathers to line their nests.

Sanderlings

A pair of sanderlings fly by and land fifty feet in front of us — their legs in perpetual motion, they feed on the first insects liberated by the melting snow.

A single purple sandpiper sits silently amid the ice and snow, his dark silhouette a sharp contrast against the bleak background. With his feathers fluffed, he occasionally pecks the ground, possibly to catch a small red spider crawling across his path. This particular short-legged sandpiper appears exhausted. Cornwallis Island may be his nesting grounds or he may have stopped only to feed and rest before continuing his journey north. Arriving from the Maritime Provinces or from as far south as the coast of Maryland, he has to wait a few more days before preparing a nest.

The purple sandpiper

In this expanse of shades of white, the solitary, starling-sized sandpiper looks out of place. His slightly downcurved bill adds to his downcast look.

But only the human mind can read this feeling of despair into the scene. The sandpiper is probably quite comfortable and content. More than likely, his mate is somewhere nearby preparing for the mating season. Soon a shallow depression on the open barrens will serve as a nest. The nest, lined with willow leaves, will contain four ground-coloured eggs that are incubated for a relatively short time.

Once hatched the downy well-camouflaged chicks will feed constantly and grow rapidly to adult size in the twenty-four-hour daylight of the arctic.

Shorebirds are so common on their wintering grounds down south no one pays any attention to them. Here, even a snow bunting is an event.

The heating system in our home-away-from-home leaves much to be desired. There are only two options — you can turn it on or off. Since it is -28°C outside we decide to turn it on. That is our first mistake. The second mistake is to sleep inside our eiderdown sleeping bags. The temperature in our room rises to 30°C. It is hard enough to sleep in full daylight; the heat makes it impossible. The next morning we head for the showers on Resolute's main street.

A Day in Resolute

Breakfast is at 7 A.M.

It is a good idea to be on time for meals in the cookhouse. Clean-up is prompt and fast, without any regard to who you are or how much influence you have with the management. The cook, a proud New-foundlander, can and does get you out of there fast — first by flinging a wet mop around your feet, then, as noisily as possible, by rearranging the furniture while you try to down the last sip of coffee. His methods are effective and based on years of experience. The cookhouse is one of the more inviting places in Resolute Bay, and people love to gather here for hours at a time sipping hot drinks and talking.

The heavy fog and falling snow that have besieged Resolute promise to keep us here another day.

A walk to the old dump site on the outskirts of town is a good way of killing time. I discover a snow bunting's nest — a definite sign of spring. A hollow in the rocky terrain has been covered by a foot-square piece of plywood and is padded with materials gathered by the female bunting.

Shorebirds are feeding along the edge of a streamlet that winds over the frozen ground. Purple and Baird's sandpipers stay just ahead of us running over the snow-free rocks and velvet-like mosses which line the streamlet's banks. A Thayer's gull flies over us in search of food.

The snow is still waist deep where it has drifted during the winter. A thin, icy crust with wet snow underneath makes walking difficult. By afternoon, more snow is falling.

We had hoped to reach Bathurst by twin Otter today, but the weather does not improve enough for even this powerful airplane.

This morning we saw the old dump site. The only other diversion is to see the new one. This we do. Stu hopes to see some ivory gulls which sometimes come to such habitats in search of food. He has banded many of these white gulls during his stay on Seymour Island the year before, and he hopes to find one of his banded birds here.

The new dump is two or three miles outside of town. We borrow a truck and after supper drive along one of the two roads leading out of Resolute Bay. The fog is dense, but we have no problems finding the site — mainly because this is the only road leading in that direction. On the way, we stop to watch a row of gulls stretched out in a one-quarter-mile-long line beside the road. We look hard for an ivory gull, but do not see any — there are only Thayer's and glaucous gulls. At the dump, more gulls, their feathers stained by garbage, fly noisily over the smouldering debris, snatching at anything edible, often on the wing, and carrying it off to a more private feeding place. A long-tailed jaeger with his aerial acrobatics keeps the gulls on the alert by snatching their tidbits away from them.

We walk about the dump searching for the elusive ivory gull. The soiled state of the birds, combined with the fog, makes identification difficult. We find no ivory gulls and Stu decides to take the other road which leads to the Eskimo village, hoping to find one there.

The gravel road contrasts with the still snow-covered landscape. Near a shallow melt pond just outside the village, we get out of our truck and scan the horizon for ivory gulls.

In the ditch beside us lies a dead dog, stiff and frozen. It is a young white dog, and appears to have been in excellent physical condition. It has been shot only recently and left to be consumed by the arctic environment. A red collar is still around his neck. Why would anyone shoot this apparently healthy animal?

Glaucous gull

Later I learn that such practices are common among the native people. Often a dog that does not meet its owner's requirements, either in performance or behaviour, is shot. To the Eskimo, a dog is a dog. It is only allowed to live as long as it is useful.

Huskies have served Eskimos for centuries. Today there are few, if any, pure-blooded huskies left. When the white man came he started to breed stronger, more powerful sled-dogs and this has resulted in the loss of much of the husky's true identity. Once grayish white, huskies now come in all colours and sizes. Nevertheless, their wolf-like appearance and hunting spirit have prevailed.

In the old days dogs were turned loose to forage for themselves during the summer months. They roamed alone or in packs and were able to survive by hunting small wild animals (lemmings were their main diet) and eating the scraps in Eskimo villages. During the winter huskies were well looked after. A daily diet of raw walrus or seal meat kept them in excellent condition.

Thayer's gulls

The husky loves cold and is probably most comfortable sleeping through a midwinter blizzard. His dense fur protects him from even the most extreme cold.

Like most dogs, the husky is usually friendly and enjoys man's company. One should, however, always approach these dogs cautiously; numerous attacks on man have been recorded and the many stories told by arctic travellers of savage dogs elicit respect in even the bravest souls. Huskies are notorious fighters, often severely injuring their harness partners. During long hungry periods they have been known to feed on their own kind. And stories are told of them eating children. A wild-running husky deserves more respect than the largest of arctic wolves.

At the Eskimo village I find what I expect to find. Wooden houses built on aboveground foundations make up the little community. A stretched polar bear skin drying on a roof of one of the small bungalows is the only visible remnant of the history of these proud and skillful people.

Before the white man came, Eskimos survived on what the arctic region had to offer. Wild game provided all their necessities — food, clothing, fuel, and housing. And their art, of necessity, has evolved from the natural mediums available to them. Their language has no word for "art," yet they have always created it.

Eskimo art has never been more popular than today, nor has there ever been as much of it. Unfortunately, there has also never been less artistry in it. Commercial pressures to produce more and more "art" have spread like a fatal white man's disease and are threatening to exterminate real Eskimo art. Quality of work has reached an all-time low; the few good works are lost amid the mass of mediocrity.

In the old days images of men and animals were carved from memory and were intended to be objects of pleasure only, or else playthings for children. A carver "released" the form of a seal or a walrus or a whale or a polar bear from a piece of ivory — initially he probably had no idea what he intended to sculpt. It was a natural and spontaneous creation. Today, Eskimo carving has become an industry.

Most of the old ways have disappeared. Housing, clothing, art, eating habits, religion — all have changed. The white man's culture has engulfed both the Eskimo and his environment.

Here and there on some remote island the odd family group still lives by the old ways. With as little contact as possible with the outside world, these groups live in the twentieth century much as their ancestors did thousands of years ago. Houses of snow (igloos) are their winter homes; tents made from animal skins are their summer shelters; dog sleds and kayaks are their means of transportation. But this way of life is rare, and survival is often reinsured by modern hunting guns.

Some of the Eskimo philosophies of life, however, have been retained, as the following story illustrates.

On one of his many expeditions in the high arctic, Stu MacDonald was trapped in a remote region by an early thaw. The way back to headquarters by dog sled was dangerous and chancy, but he asked one of the local Eskimos if he would guide him back to civilization. The Eskimo hesitated for a moment, then briefly consulted with his family before answering. The answer was yes, he would guide Stu back, but he added, simply and without any visible emotion, "We may die." Death is an accepted part of daily life here — there is no fear of death, only fear of suffering.

Our excursion through the Eskimo village ends my first whole day in the arctic. Snow, fog, and ice prevent us once again from reaching Bathurst Island.

On to Bathurst Island

We spend the morning walking around the outskirts of town.

More and more shorebirds are gathering along the creeks and ever-growing melt ponds. The stripped remains of an ill-fated airplane lie partially submerged in the middle of one of the larger ponds. One sees many such skeletons, and they are not a welcome invitation to arctic flying.

Throughout the day the sun makes only brief appearances through the dense fog. Meals at the local cookhouse are the highlights of our day. The weather does not improve and by evening we are resigned to another night in Resolute. I must admit I am getting tired of Resolute Bay; only the constant hope of getting away makes the mud and damp of this drab little town bearable. On the credit side, the fog, the barren ground, and the hilltops often visible only as blurred shadows, provide me with fascinating backgrounds for imaginary wildlife paintings.

Late in the evening, much to our surprise, word comes that we can leave at once by twin Otter.

While crossing the sea ice I see my first seals. They lie motionless along a crack in the ice, basking and drying their dense fur in the spring sun, which now and then penetrates through the patchy cloud cover.

Two hours later we land. There is great commotion on the high ridge that serves as an airstrip at the Bathurst camp. A noisy snow-mobile takes away oil drums and personal gear. The roar of the plane's engines adds to the hustle and bustle, the almost city-like atmosphere.

But once the plane vanishes from sight over a far hilltop there is only silence. It is cold and windy. As I look around, I see the sun reflecting off frozen snow and icy windswept ponds. In all directions there is only desolation. The cry of a knot on a distant ridge momentarily gives some life to the scene.

Here at last is the Bathurst Island camp.

It has been built high on a ridge overlooking the great Polar Bear Pass Valley to the south and the Good Sir River to the east. Next to the air strip stands the laboratory building. With its second storey obser-vation tower and a Canadian flag fluttering in the wind, it is the most imposing building in the camp. Farther along the ridge are four canvas-covered parcoll huts, one fibreglass igloo, and an outhouse. That is all.

The parcolls, our living quarters, are surprisingly comfortable. These half-circular, double-insulated canvas, aluminum-framed struc-tures even have wooden floors, oil stoves, and comfortable beds — practically all the comforts of home.

The igloo is the storehouse. It is made of fibreglass to protect its contents from prowling animals. Within, there is enough food to keep two people alive for twelve months.

The muskox head is placed under the flag at the laboratory, in such a way that it overlooks Polar Bear Pass.

Michael McNall has been here for several weeks and he is anxious to show me around. He is studying the jaeger population and examin-ing prospective nesting sites.

Glaucous gull ▶

It must be midnight when we start our walk into Polar Bear Pass. Sun, silence, and heat shimmers rising off the hilltops. I wonder whether it is all a mirage.

We follow a gentle slope into the valley. From time to time the flight of a knot and black-bellied plover and the cry of a long-tailed jaeger break the silence. Two greater snow geese fly by and vanish as quickly as they came. A pair of king eider ducks fly low over the valley floor, no doubt searching for open water — still a rare commodity here. Spring, apparently, is two weeks late, and the birds which have come to nest on Bathurst have had a hard time establishing nesting sites and finding enough food among the lingering ice and snow.

We walk around examining snow-free moss-covered mounds for signs of mating jaegers, and it is one o'clock in the morning before we get back to camp.

Ringed seals on pack ice ▶

From the observation tower we see three caribou and several musk oxen feeding on distant slopes. (As it turns out these caribou are the only ones I see during my stay in the arctic.) Presumably they are Peary's caribou since this species is often found on eastern high arctic islands. Although never as plentiful as their cousins which migrate by the thousands through other parts of the Canadian arctic, they are particularly scarce this year. Three or four years ago a hard winter killed off many caribou and musk oxen. A heavy early snowfall melted, then froze again overnight, lining the gound with a hard layer of porcelain-like ice that made it impossible for most animals to scratch through to the underlying vegetation.

Exploring the Arctic

First, breakfast. The smell of sizzling bacon and freshly brewed coffee fills the air, spreading a welcome mat no one could resist. This, my first meal in the Bathurst camp, is relaxing and leisurely. With no harassed cook hurrying us along, discussions of wildlife observations go on and on. I soon feel part of this little group of arctic travellers, and their goodwill and good humor make me feel welcome.

Only my new boots, still in perfect condition, give me away as the greenhorn I am. (But I am glad to see that Stu's boots are also brand new and he has been travelling in the high arctic for more than twenty years.)

After breakfast everyone goes off in different directions, each searching for his particular species of wildlife.

I walk about nearby slopes and ridges looking for life of any kind. Now and then glaucous and Thayer's gulls fly overhead. Long-tailed jaegers soar by providing constant entertainment. I am fascinated by the bleak yet hauntingly beautiful countryside, but my attempts to draw birds are spoiled by the brisk north wind and the wet snow which soon covers both my sketch pad and all of Bathurst Island.

But there are signs of life and of spring. Lichens and mosses — purple, red, yellow, and brown — on snow-free rocks and on high ground. In the distance snow and fog, but when the sun breaks through the cloud cover the landscape is aglow with warm shades of cream and violet blue.

Distances here are deceptive. When I think I am almost back in camp, it turns out to be several miles away.

There is no official lunch. Everyone forages for himself. Some take their lunch with them on their daily travels, which means they can range farther from camp to see and investigate more of the island.

Long-tailed jaegers

East of camp there is an area known as "Stonehenge," a group of large stones scattered on a long slope. I hope to go there after lunch, but after walking two miles or more, Stonehenge is still a long way off. But Stonehenge's rocks have become bigger and as I have little else to do, I keep on walking in zigzags along ridges and through valleys. The valleys are still covered with deep wet snow and it is heavy going. My built-in time clock keeps telling me that it will soon be dark and that I must return to camp. Of course darkness never comes. I never do reach my objective — an unexpected encounter with a pair of rock ptarmigans takes up most of the afternoon.

I see the male ptarmigan long before the female. From a distance he blends perfectly into the snowy terrain. When I get close, he struts before me like a rooster in a barnyard. At times he lowers his head, tilts his body, and runs ahead for several yards. Then he stops, stretches his neck, and tilts his body in a more upright position, looking at me in an offended but dignified manner.

Rock ptarmigan

This game goes on for some time. During one of these displays, I spot the female. I think it is the highlight or reflection in her eyes that first gives her away. She is huddling in a patch of wet grass surrounded by snow. As I approach she gets up and follows the male on one of his runs.

Now it gets quite exciting. The male flies up twenty feet or more into the air, chattering loudly. He then glides back to the ground and struts about, letting me know in no uncertain terms that this is his domain. For an hour or more he repeats his charade. The female stays several feet ahead of me at all times, running or walking over the snow and sitting on the small patches of bare ground, obviously hoping that I will lose sight of her.

The female has changed to summer plumage. The densely mottled feathers on her head, breast, and back provide her with almost perfect camouflage among the wet grasses, melt puddles, and small rocks. Only her belly feathers, the primaries in the wings, and the feathers insulating her legs and feet are white.

The male is white. His outer tail feathers are black, but are usually well hidden, and visible only when he fans his tail feathers while courting. The combs over his eyes are swollen because it is the mating season. They are a vermilion red, or, as Stu MacDonald describes them, "as no other red on earth."

Walking on Bathurst Island is an extraordinary experience. There is only the constant wind and the odd cry of a distant shorebird to keep me company. Skeletal remains of musk oxen and caribou lie scattered here and there. Deserted lemming burrows that perforate snow-free earth mounds bear witness to the lemming crash of the winter before. The rest is desolation.

On the way back to camp I have to cross the Good Sir River. The shore and river bed are lined with sand and pebbles. There is still no free water flowing; for the most part the river bed is covered with snow and walking through the Good Sir is a challenge. It is hard to tell whether I am walking on ice covered by snow or whether the snow is two inches or two feet deep. I cautiously cross large patches of snow, and, just as I think I've made it out of the river bed, I sink chest deep into the white stuff.

My first reaction is simply to climb out. But as soon as I move my legs and feet (which is difficult enough), I sink deeper. With my hands and arms I push as much snow as possible away from my body, thus preparing a good-sized hole around me in case I slip farther down. I keep digging snow, one handful at a time, away from me until I reach my knees.

Now I am able to at least move more freely. I compact the snow around me with my hands, knees, and feet, and build a fairly solid platform from which I can make my escape. I do sink another foot or so, but this is nothing since my burrow is now large and there is little danger that I will suddenly disappear beneath the snow. Step by step, I crawl out of the snow to the safety of the more solid river bank. I have learned a lot about arctic snow and snowdrifts today.

Looking for Caribou and Musk Oxen

We are to go on an aerial survey of the caribou and musk oxen on Bathurst Island. At 10 A.M. Mel Veau, our single Otter pilot, lands on the Bathurst camp airstrip. Janet Rowell, David Gill, Stu MacDonald, and I are to be the spotters. Equipped with binoculars, we are to scan the landscape for musk oxen and caribou.

The most exciting part of this venture is the takeoff. Even Stu, the most experienced among us, agrees afterwards that it could have been disastrous. What happens is this: the plane, with its engine wide open and vibrating in every part, barrels down the uneven runway. Suddenly the wheels hit a snowbank, sending the Otter leaping into the air. The impact slows our speed considerably and we are once again earthbound. Still moving at the same speed, the plane skids and bumps along the rough terrain heading downhill towards the end of the ridge. Luckily, Mel retains enough speed to become airborne just before the plane reaches the end of the slope.

There is a sigh of relief and a period of silence.

After our initial adventure it is fair flying all the way. The weather is good and the visibility excellent. Only an occasional fog patch gets between us and the barren ground below.

Most of Bathurst Island is still covered with snow. Some hilltops are bare, revealing the warm browns and reds of a reawakening vegetation. But lakes and rivers are frozen solid and where wind has swept away the snow the turquoise-green of frozen water can be seen.

Along some rivers and streams green-brown patches hint that the melt has begun. At times the countryside is hilly, and the canyons and gulleys below make fascinating viewing.

We see no caribou, even though Stu spots fresh caribou tracks in the snow. Musk oxen are also scarce. We see three herds; the largest consists of only ten animals. We circle over these ten, desperately searching for a calf. We do not see one. In fact, no calves at all have been seen this year.

Snowy owls

I am fascinated by the musk oxen and the speed with which they form their defensive circle. It is hard to believe that these stocky, short-legged animals can move with such grace and speed — gathering together, instinctively defending themselves against our noisy airplane.

Our landing back at camp early in the afternoon is smoother than our takeoff. Over a cup of tea in the cook parcoll, we discuss what we have seen. I decide that my eyes need more training — a flock of snow geese is all I have seen, besides the three musk ox herds. From his side of the airplane Stu has seen many more snow geese and one snowy owl. All in all, it has been slim pickings.

I spend the rest of the day walking about the countryside within two miles of camp. Three snow geese fly by, honking as they disappear in the distance. A pair of knots fly to and fro from their feeding areas in the wetlands of Polar Bear Pass to the stony ridges to the north of the valley, their distant calls echoing over the landscape.

Birds and Lemmings

Today is the first truly sunny day. The combination of bright arctic sun and strong wind melts the snow at a great rate. The terrain changes. Melt ponds form in the valley; lichen, mosses, and patches of purple saxifrage burst into bloom. Even the arctic willows show signs of life. Their stunted branches, crawling along the ground, yesterday looked like deformed snakes in need of food; today they sprout buds. Overnight spring has arrived. (There must be something in the story told to everyone when they first arrive in the arctic. It concerns a worker on an oil rig who writes home saying he hopes that summer will fall on a weekend next year, so he can have it off.)

The valley below camp, Polar Bear Pass, comes to life. Black-bellied plovers, golden plovers, knots, pectoral sandpipers, king eider ducks, greater snow geese, and old squaw ducks who have been arriving in small numbers throughout the wetlands, are suddenly all here. There is great activity everywhere, and the silence has been broken by birds displaying their different courtship behaviors; it is a good time for intensive bird watching.

Several pairs of long-tailed jaegers pay constant visits to our cook parcoll hoping for leftovers. These are rarely offered. The idea, of course, is that the people working here on behavioral studies observe these creatures under natural conditions. (That long-tailed jaegers have been fed on fried bacon or salami would not make good reading in a scientific journal.)

Red-throated loon ▶

Thayer's or glaucous gulls sit at the edge of the ridge facing the cookhouse. They, too, have only one thing in mind — food.

To see a glaucous gull gliding in the wind over the Good Sir River is a sight to behold. Almost effortlessly, this large gull weaves back and forth over the patchy countryside. Riding the wind, it can suddenly make an about face and with great speed fade into the horizon. From a distance the pale blue and white of these birds blend perfectly with their background.

Thayer's gulls

I spend the morning observing shorebirds — jaegers, gulls, and anything else I can feast my eyes on.

I am determined to find a lemming. This proves to be no easy task and I finally decide to follow David Gill's trapline hoping to find at least a trapped animal which I can use as a model for future reference.

◀ *Caribou*

This, too, proves unsuccessful. There are no lemmings and only their frozen burrows are proof they ever existed. Later I learn that very few have been captured this spring, and their numbers have certainly not increased since.

Golden plovers

A lemming population goes through a four-year cycle. Every four years it reaches a peak. Then, for some unknown reason, all lemmings suddenly vanish. There is no sign even of their bodies — nothing — they just disappear. Fortunately, each of the eastern high arctic islands has its own four-year lemming cycle which does not necessarily coincide with the others'. And while there has obviously been a lemming crash on Bathurst Island this year, the lemming population on other, nearby islands may still be high.

Few snowy owls have been seen on Bathurst Island this spring — a result of the lemming crash. Lemmings are the snowy owl's main food source; the owls have moved on to some other island where they can survive and rear their young.

Rock ptarmigans ▶

Jaegers also depend on lemmings for food, particularly when they first arrive on their breeding grounds. Although the jaegers here are now "plover feeding" on small insects, it is doubtful if this year there is enough food for them to raise their young.

The trapline leads me over the ridges north of camp. A fox den has been reported some two or three miles farther on, but I decide to make that another day's excursion.

David Gill's traps have been set along the edge of the snow line where lemmings are most likely to surface in order to escape their water-filled burrows. Many, in fact most traps, are set deep in the snow. The snow here is still much deeper than around camp, and the spring-like sights and sounds I saw earlier this morning are absent. It is as if I have suddenly crossed back into midwinter.

The lonely call of a jaeger and the constant wind rustling through my parka are again the only sounds.

I return to camp late in the afternoon without having seen a lemming.

Michael McNall and I try to record some bird sounds, without much success.

The night is sunny and the wind has subsided. The valley below camp is still and once again deserted. What has happened to all the wildlife which only this morning filled the air with sounds and sights of spring? There is only a single pair of black-bellied plovers acting out a courtship flight. The calm, the midnight sun, and the peace of the arctic night are appealing and tranquilizing.

Musk oxen ▶

An Encounter with an Arctic Fox

All of Bathurst Island is bathed in bright sunshine. It is the longest day of the year, June 21, but at this high latitude it makes little difference to us. All days are equally long and I find the complete absence of darkness still hard to get used to. My activities have always been planned by the clock of light and dark, and my system demands certain things at certain times. Hardest of all is to climb into bed and sleep in bright sunshine. Luckily, the brisk arctic air and my long walks usually resolve this problem.

This morning my walk leads me along the top of some ridges west of camp. Six snow geese fly by, moving in a northerly direction and flying over the valley floor at approximately the height of the hilltops on which I am walking. At eye level I get a fantastic view of their wings in motion.

Soon after I see my first arctic fox. He has started to change into his summer fur and is part white, part brown. His head and hindquarters have lost most of their dense white winter fur and he looks scruffy.

He stays well ahead. From time to time he stops and turns around to look at me, then trots off again. He is a long way from his den; his hunt has led him into Polar Bear Pass in search of shorebird nests. With the low lemming population, the Bathurst Island foxes, too, have a hard time surviving.

◄ *Arctic fox*

These little foxes are well adapted to their harsh environment and they are expert hunters. Their olfactory organs are so developed they can smell out a lemming nest buried deep under the snow. Often one can see an arctic fox carefully combing a hillside, back and forth, back and forth, not missing a square foot of it. With his nose to the ground, he will search out any nest and soon deprive it of eggs and hatchlings. Once a nest has been found, whether it be a shorebird's, a jaeger's, or that of a greater snow goose, it is almost always destroyed.

An arctic fox snatches one egg at a time. Some are eaten immediately, others are carefully taken and buried, to be dug up later when fresh food is hard to find.

Many eggs and young birds never reach maturity because of the arctic fox's cunning. Researchers curse the arctic fox who can within moments destroy their research projects — an observer may have spent weeks watching and documenting the progress of a nest, only to have it completely wiped out in seconds by one of the little foxes.

Like all living things in the high arctic, the fox population goes through cycles. Mostly dependent on lemmings, the number of foxes in any area varies greatly from year to year. At the height of the lemming population explosion, foxes are numerous and their hunting territories may be quite small.

When lemmings are scarce, foxes must cover large hunting territories. Many starve to death and few young are raised. If conditions are extremely bad, no young at all will be raised that year.

It is still too early to tell whether or not a litter will be raised in the occupied den a few miles from camp, but the adults are surviving and appear to be healthy. My colleagues, who have been to the den, are sure that it is occupied. Apparently by imitating a fox bark and directing it down the fox burrow, they always get a response. (*Note:* Several months later I learned that a litter of young foxes had indeed been raised in the den. I was told that one of the young had adopted the camp area and, when last seen, was licking the bacon fat off some rocks after a kitchen clean-up. But lemmings had not increased significantly by fall and the young foxes will be hard pressed to survive the long period of darkness and cold that lies ahead.)

The landscape keeps changing. In the valley, rivers and ponds are filling with melt water where a few days ago all was still frozen solid and covered with snow. Here and there creeklets have begun to feed the riverbed of Good Sir, changing the colour of the snow which lines its banks. More and more purple saxifrage is bursting into bloom. In midsummer these patches of purple scattered over the slopes and hilltops must be a sight to behold.

Suddenly the sun disappears and a raging snowstorm engulfs me.

Lemmings

That evening I finally see my first lemming. It has been captured in a live trap by David Gill, and it has no fear of humans whatsoever. When I put my hand into the small wire cage, it promptly walks up my hand and arm, and, with whiskers twitching, sniffs my shirt.

A couple of quick pencil sketches are all I can make of this constantly moving model. I don't think he even stays in one place long enough to look for a means of escape from his cage. Back and forth, around and around, up and down he goes. Every three seconds he attacks the wire mesh of the cage with his modified forefoot, creating an irritating sound resembling an alarm clock bell.

His adaptation to the long winter takes place in the claws on his forefeet. Each fall the middle claws of each forefoot grow into paddle-like structures designed for digging through thick, icy snowbanks. In spring this remarkable growth stops, and the claws wear down to normal size.

Our lemming's fur has changed to its summer colour — many shades of brown. Some light gray or white is still visible on its back. In winter the collared lemming changes to white, a perfect camouflage.

The Birds Arrive

As on other mornings, after breakfast everyone gathers his gear and strikes off in different directions. I head downhill in the deep wet snow lining the slopes of the camp ridge, trying to retrace my footprints of the day before — easier to do than making new ones. Often the footprints are knee deep, making the uphill climb strenuous, especially after a Bathurst Island breakfast.

A pair of snow geeese fly by, breaking the morning silence. I now expect to see at least one pair every day. So far, they have not disappointed me.

After walking for thirty minutes, my first stop is a small pond which has formed overnight. Nearby, an earth hummock, where snowy owls have nested the year before, makes a perfect observation platform. The moss-covered earth mound is still littered with owl "pellets" and white owl feathers. Lemming skulls and bones are scattered here and there. It is not a tidy spot, but the soft thick moss covering looks comfortable, and I sit down to rest.

Ten minutes later a pair of king eider ducks suddenly appear and land on the shallow water of the melt pond. My presence does not worry them. They begin to dip for food, preen and ruffle their feathers, and make themselves at home.

By approaching the ducks two or three steps at a time, then pausing for a minute or so, I get within twenty feet of them. But by the time I reach the edge of the pond both male and female have settled on the opposite shore in the wet grass.

Their journey to Bathurst Island has been a long one, and they have come to the melt pond to feed and rest before building their nest.

The female buries her bill in her scapular feathers and appears to drowse. The male stands guard, keeping a close watch on me. His brilliant yet gentle colours could only have been invented by nature, and his plumage is intensified even more by the morning's sunshine.

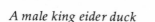

A male king eider duck

King eider ducks spend much of their time feeding along the edge of the northern coast wherever they can find open water. Here, during the fall and winter months, they gather in large groups. In early spring when the days become longer, they separate and migrate inland to the most remote of arctic islands in search of small freshwater ponds. Often a single pair will arrive in a still-frozen land searching desperately for a suitable nesting ground.

The nest of the king eider is often nothing but a hollow depression lined with eiderdown. It may be on flat tundra, on the slope of a hillside, or on top of a ridge some distance from the nearest pond.

The female's plumage is such that it blends almost perfectly with the surrounding landscape. When sitting on a nest, a female king eider is almost invisible and will not abandon her brood until a predator is within striking range.

The male stays away from the nest; with his brilliant colours flashing, he makes himself the target for any nest robber.

King eider ducks do not congregate in large breeding colonies — nests are scattered here and there. Often a mile or more separates one nest from another.

I spend most of the morning watching the eiders feeding and relaxing in and around the tiny melt pond.

Later I walk farther into Polar Bear Pass and see shorebirds feeding. Walking is becoming more and more difficult — dry ground is at a premium, and only on some of the higher earth hummocks can I occasionally avoid the mud and cold melt water. But even these hummocks are not safe to sit and rest on for any length of time. Their thick, velvet-like moss covering is swollen with melt water.

Like a thirsty sponge, the moss has absorbed the surrounding icy water — something not always immediately detectable. I often get up just after having sat down, when the icy water penetrates my jeans in a vulnerable spot. To be soaked to the knees has become common-place, and each walk requires a change of clothing. But there is some comfort in this — one has to change only from the waist down, unless something unforeseen happens, such as slipping in the mud or tripping over a hidden boulder and landing face down in the nearest melt pond.

Sloshing around in these wetlands keeps the laundry bill down. My new blue jeans have already faded to a pale, pale blue. My shoes, too, are now much more respectable. They have acquired a number of wrinkles across their uppers and have curled up nicely from being dried beside the hot stove in our parcoll. And there is hardly any need to wash my heavy woolen socks by the conventional method. They are thoroughly dunked many times each day.

King eiders—male and female

The sunshine of the morning disappears by noon. A gentle snow-fall covers the valley, obscuring the distant hilltops.

These weather changes are remarkable. It is never a good idea to count on anything weatherwise — sunshine can quickly give way to fog, rain, hail, or snow. Calm is always shortlived; the strong arctic wind drones on and on.

After lunch I return to the same pond. Although quite small, it is still one of the largest unfrozen ponds for miles around. When I arrive, there are no signs of life at all, but soon an old squaw drake appears and sits down on the icy water. His landing is not as graceful as that of the king eiders — he approaches and plops down heavily.

Long-tailed jaeger ▶

His flight course is much higher than that of the eiders and his approach more erratic, as if he has noticed the pond only at the last moment. Almost immediately, he sees me, ruffles his feathers once or twice, and is off again disappearing over the still-frozen Good Sir River. Unlike the old squaw ducks I have seen floating about during the winter months in the more southern harbors of the Great Lakes, these breeding ducks are very wary.

The only other visitor is a black-bellied plover, a male. The black and white pattern is distinct; in female birds the division between black and white is blurred.

The plover spends some time feeding in the wet grasses surrounding the melt pond. His reflection in the pond is magnificent. In full sunshine, his back becomes a warm, creamy white almost totally obscuring the black and white blotchy wing patterns so characteristic of the species.

These plovers are a common sight during the spring and summer months. That single male has probably built a nest nearby on drier ground, and his mate is probably sitting on the nest, incubating or still laying eggs. The nest is a shallow depression in the ground, camouflaged by stones, mosses, and perhaps a brilliant purple patch of saxifrage.

I sit on the owl hill near the melt pond for a long time; the sky constantly changes the mood of the landscape. But I see no more shorebirds or ducks. Sitting among the remains of the owl's nest I imagine the ghostly silhouette of a snowy owl. Several have probably landed on that very hill this year, only to find no food. The land is empty of owls and lemmings; but their signs are everywhere — burrows, skeletons, feathers.

Later I walk through the valley of Polar Bear Pass past the campsite and sit on a distant ridge watching three jaegers performing their aerial acrobatics over the water-soaked valley below. Noisily they chase one another diving and soaring, disappearing in a low-hanging fog cloud only to reappear at a higher altitude.

◀ *Golden plover*

BUERSCHAPER '76

The evening's meal is one to remember. A turkey has been liberated from the deep freeze and prepared with all the trimmings. (We have had a snowfall today, so why not a Christmas feast?) Only, it is June. This bothers me a little.

After dinner, the observation tower. The night sun is bright, all clouds have disappeared, longer shadows appear on the hillsides. Where there is snow, the shadows are cobalt blue; where the ground is bare, the shadows are raw umber. Heat shimmers rising from the awakening ground cast mirage-like scenes miles from where I am sitting. It reminds me of that first night when I sat in the observation tower looking at the caribou grazing. At midnight the sun is still bright and the sky a multitude of blues.

◀ *Sanderling*

Weasels and Courtship Ceremonies

Today is bright and sunny. Once again I visit the small melt pond. An old squaw drake flies up from the pond long before I reach its shores, but an hour or more passes and I see no more birds.

Back at camp a weasel has been captured. It is a beautiful creature— its back a soft raw umber, the underside of its neck a pale lemon-lime, and creamy white fur lines its stomach. This particular weasel had been hunting for lemmings in burrows on the side of the camp ridge, more successfully than I, for he had captured one.

Weasels live among the lichen-covered rocks and are not usually seen around campsites. The dead lemming is as large as the weasel. Although its body is shorter, the lemming appears to be bulkier than its hunter.

The weasel has been captured in a live trap and it has taken four people to do it. Only by blowing cigarette smoke down one of the many lemming burrows in the hillside and by blocking all other burrows with hands, rocks, and wire cages, did the animal finally surrender. Once in the wire cage he injured himself trying to escape through the wire mesh, and the only thing to do was put the animal out of its misery. Both the weasel and the lemming are now scientific specimens.

Later in the morning I sit on a hillside soaking up the sun and watching pectoral sandpipers during their courtship flight. The male pectoral sandpiper has developed a unique adaptation. By inflating his throat and neck with air, he greatly expands them, and, while in flight, releases this air, creating a sound difficult to describe. It resembles most closely the European type of ambulance siren, a weird sound indeed.

Time and time again these pectoral sandpipers fly high into the air, at times disappearing from sight. Then, on a declining flight, they streak by, eventually landing on the valley floor below my vantage point; the male behind the female, projecting his strange sound loud and clear. According to Stu, few have the opportunity to witness this particular courtship behavior, but to me the sound of a pectoral sandpiper is as much a part of Bathurst Island as the ice and snow.

The valley floor of Polar Bear Pass is flooded from end to end. Ponds, puddles, and creeklets are rapidly swelling with melt water. During my afternoon hike, my friend, the old squaw drake, is again floating on Eider Pond (the little melt pond next to the Good Sir River) and, as always, he flies off long before I reach the edge of the pond.

Along the bottom of the camp ridge a pair of golden plovers is busily feeding among patches of grass not yet submerged by melt water. A single knot follows them whenever they move to a new feeding ground.

The pectoral sandpipers are still noisily performing their courtship ceremony.

A solitary knot

Distant pools, ponds, and puddles in the lower valley are teeming with waterfowl. One of the larger of the countless mini-lakes is inhabited by six king eider ducks, two red-throated loons, and many red phalaropes. These sites draw me like magnets. Getting soaked is of no consequence, and distance has lost all significance. But walking has become very difficult. The remaining snow and ice bridges linking melt ponds have been undermined by the frigid melt water and occasionally they give way as I scramble over them in search of drier ground. On such occasions, only fast and fancy footwork can save my cameras, binoculars, and sketch pads.

Male and female common eiders

Zigzagging back and forth across the wetlands, I try with each hazardous step to come closer to any form of wildlife which is at first often only a moving dot on the horizon. Not until the return trip to camp, when much energy has been spent slushing about the sponge-wet ground, do I realize how far I have travelled, and usually not before several miles of open tundra have been crisscrossed and the camp buildings high on the ridge look like tiny huts, blurred by the heat shimmers rising from the hilltops.

The way back is twice as difficult. Several rest stations are necessary during these long, soggy walks.

During one rest stop two snow geese appear out of nowhere and land in a nearby pool. The pond is still surrounded by ice and snow, and the colors reflecting off those great white birds are something to see — blue, turquoise, yellow, bounce off their sculptured bodies. At times their undersides appear brighter than their backs, so intense and vibrant are they.

Greater snow geese

The geese preen their feathers and feed on the grasses submerged by the melt water. Their head feathers are stained a rusty-red from the iron in the water.

Greater snow geese usually arrive in the high arctic in early June after a long flight up the Eastern Seaboard. They rest at Cap Tour-mente, Quebec. Thousands then fly farther north over Ungava and disperse into single pairs in search of nesting grounds on the islands of the high arctic. The Bathurst Island population of snow geese has been arriving, one pair at a time, for days.

Today, it seems that they are all here. Some small ponds are inhabited by as many as eight geese. They are resting, feeding, and enjoying the sun that gleams and sparkles off the wetlands of Polar Bear Pass.

The sun stays with us and the outdoors is so tantalizing that a third walk into the wetlands is necessary.

Numerous pairs of king eider ducks have gathered in the flooded valley below camp. A pair of king eiders float leisurely on Eider Pond. A pair of old squaw ducks land briefly, but, as usual, they disappear quickly as though spooked.

Arctic Spring

Mike McNall and I are on kitchen duty today. It is our turn to be the first to get up, heat the cook parcoll, and prepare breakfast.

Our morning meal consists of fresh coffee or tea, French toast, and fried bacon. Our recipe for French toast is simple. A dozen eggs are broken into a bowl and scrambled. Slices of white bread are submerged in the scrambled raw egg, then fried to a golden brown in heavy cast-iron pans. Served piping hot and decorated with two or three slices of fried bacon, our dish gets nothing but compliments. Flipping the egg-coated bread slices high over the stove even merits an occasional burst of applause. Seconds are available; most important to Jamie, aged sixteen, who has a healthy appetite.

After breakfast Stu and I walk across the Good Sir River. We cross just north of camp and head towards Eeyore Hill. This landmark has been so named when an old bull musk ox died on the hill in the spring of 1968. According to Stu, a huge old musk ox appeared on the hilltop one day and stood there alone for several days, then slumped to the ground and died.

To witness a natural death is rare in the arctic. Most animals fall victim to predators when weakened by age or disease.

In contrast to Eeyore, Stu tells me of the death of another bull musk ox near our camp. One day members of the 1968 camp crew saw a large, mature arctic wolf killing a full grown, healthy bull. The wolf attacked the musk ox time and time again until finally the ox dropped to the ground, weak from loss of blood. One more grasp of the powerful jaws and the ox was dead. The wolf then proceeded to eat his fill, staining his face with blood, which earned him the name "Old Blood Face." Apparently, he still roams Bathurst Island.

Musk oxen

We rest briefly on top of Eeyore Hill. Patches of purple saxifrage are the only signs of life. The hilltop is barren, its stony soil incapable of sustaining anything but saxifrage and arctic willow.

This is ptarmigan country and we search for a nest, both on the hilltop and on the gentle slope leading into a sheltered valley, but do not find one. The female is so well camouflaged that we would practically have to bump into her to find her.

The valley below Eeyore Hill is wet. Small creeks and the occasional tiny pond have formed since I visited the area a few days before. On the far east side near a small melt pond, a pair of greater snow geese have nested — one of them is sitting on the nest, the other is drifting about the pond.

A male ptarmigan resting on an earth hummock draws our attention. His plumage is white but stained by the muddy soil of his habitat. We get within twenty feet of him before he flies off for a few yards and lands on another hummock. It is obvious he is protecting his mate and trying to lead us away from the nest. I am sure that this is my friend of several days ago. Today he looks smaller and humbler. He seems subdued, but happy he has proliferated his species.

Among the wet grasses and small snow patches we find the remains of an arctic fox. All that is left are bits of dense white fur scattered about and a bushy white fox tail lying partially submerged in a puddle. Stu thinks that a wolf has caused its demise the previous winter. When food is hard to get, only the strongest and toughest survive.

We leave the valley, climbing a long slope to the top of the ridge on the south side, walking around a snow goose nest so as not to disturb it. Despite our concern, an arctic fox will probably rob the nest before the eggs hatch.

While crossing one of the partially frozen creeks, I break through the ice and somehow wedge one foot solidly under the broken ice. I am caught in a trap and cannot move. To free my foot I have to remove my boot. Dancing about on one foot on the water-covered ice, desperately trying to retrieve my lost boot strikes my companion as extremely funny.

By the time we reach the top of the ridge, a rest is in order. The sky is cloudy and the wind blows briskly out of the east while we sit contemplating the desolate terrain below. Behind us a bright fluorescent red steel rod has been pounded into the frozen ground by a survey crew studying the arctic soil. It looks out of place, an ugly, irritating sight. And from the wolf and fox droppings at the base of the post, it is obvious what the wildlife of Bathurst Island think of this object.

Around 2 P.M. we reach our destination, an area called the "Blow Out" where the Good Sir River floods the valley of Polar Bear Pass forming numerous puddles and ponds. Each spring geese, ducks, and shorebirds gather here to rest and feed.

Musk oxen have also been feeding here. Stu points out the free-floating grasses that have been scratched loose by their hoofs while digging through the winter snow cover in search of food.

Red phalarope

The ponds are filled with king eider ducks and red phalaropes. The eiders are skittish and cannot be approached any closer than forty or fifty yards. The red phalaropes, however, practically run over our feet. We imitate their call; they then seem to relax in our presence.

The odd pair of old squaw ducks also floats about the wetlands, but true to form they keep their distance.

Later in the afternoon, the cloud cover breaks and short periods of sunshine turn the melt ponds different colours. Where the ice still floats under melt water, warm yellow reflects on the surface. Where the wind ripples a pond's surface, deep cobalt and sky blue reflect on the surrounding snow, ice, and grasses.

Some melt pools are completely free of ice and snow, and, surrounded by the dead grass of the year before, make ideal feeding areas.

In one such pool a red phalarope sits, submerged to its belly feathers, gently pecking at the water and the surrounding grasses. At times this pond is a light, light blue, reflecting the open sky, and only the inverted image of the phalarope casts a dark blue reflection directly below the bird's rusty-red body.

Red phalaropes feeding on a melt pond

Red phalaropes are often seen swimming about like ducks on the melt ponds. The female is noticeably larger than the male. She is also the indisputable boss. She does lay the eggs, but the male incubates them. Should he decide to leave the nest, he is chastised and forced back in no uncertain terms. The female is more brightly coloured and is by far the more aggressive of the two.

Nests are built out of various bits of vegetation carried to a drier area on the open tundra near a melt pond. Four eggs usually make a clutch, producing young by early July. The chicks grow rapidly and fly south with the adult birds in early autumn.

Blow Out is busy. King eider ducks come and go, flying low over the soggy terrain; old squaws fly around in search of mates, food, or a place to rest.

The sun is shining and there is not a cloud to be seen. A long-tailed jaeger and a glaucous gull ride the wind currents over the Good Sir, occasionally sweeping by the cook parcoll in search of food.

An Unusual Calm

The morning is uneventful and relaxing. My venture into the west produces few wildlife sightings. The sun is bright and strong, the sky a vivid blue, and a moderate wind blows over the countless ponds of Polar Bear Pass, constantly changing their texture and color. Many king eiders still float about. Here and there, a plover flies over the wetlands. Otherwise a calm has beset the area.

The afternoon is much the same. Very little wildlife can be seen, only the cries of jaegers and gulls break the silence.

Dave Gill and I sit on the slope just below camp, occasionally comparing notes about museum life, but mostly we are silent, soaking up the sun and watching the valley below. Heat shimmers dance in the distance creating a blurred view. Suddenly Dave Gill rises, says "I don't think the bus is coming," and disappears over the ridge.

I walk along the bank of the Good Sir River. Melt water is gathering in its bed, and in the centre is a small creek-like current which will soon be a great rush of water. A pair of king eider ducks move about on drier ground not far from the river's edge. Searching for the perfect spot for a nest, the female waddles from spot to spot, sitting for two or three minutes in one place, then trying another. The male follows, but at a distance. I think he wants to distract my attention away from his mate.

Back at camp the calm and inactive countryside is the main topic of conversation.

The reason for the inactivity is simply that the birds of Bathurst Island have established their nests and are busy tending to their obligations.

Mike McNall has found his parasitic jaeger's nest deep in a marsh in almost the same spot where a pair of parasitic jaegers nested last year. Perhaps the same pair has returned. He has also found the remains of one of last year's young that did not make the journey south. The remains are well preserved and still frozen; the young jaeger had reached full size and learned to fly, only to be killed by a falcon. The red band encircling one of its legs proves it to be a chick of the 1975 brood.

Today has been the warmest day so far—the temperature reaches a high of 10°C. But towards evening the wind starts to blow and clouds move in from the east.

A Rainy Day in Camp

Yesterday's weather was too good to last. This morning we wake to driving rain and sleet. The oil stove has run out of fuel during the night and it is hard to crawl out of my warm eiderdown sleeping bag this dreary morning. The temperature has dropped back to just above freezing, and a dismal atmosphere prevails.

The rain and sleet stop, but the wind howls and howls around our canvas-covered buildings. Most of us stay indoors all day catching up on notes, mail, and personal chores.

Outside, the heavy cloud cover breaks from time to time, lighting up distant hilltops. The valley below appears misty, wet, and empty. To the west, the "Great Lake" I have heard so much about has now almost formed, and it is true—it is a lake. Through the scope in the observation tower I watch king eider ducks and a flock of thirteen snow geese feeding on the distant ponds of Polar Bear Pass, and golden and black-bellied plovers on the wetlands. One glaucous and several Thayer's gulls have adopted the cook parcoll area.

Each evening shortly before supper, most of us gather in the laboratory building to listen to radio broadcasts. All expeditions or field stations operating in the eastern arctic broadcast via portable radios weather conditions and other information to the main station at the Polar Continental Shelf Project headquarters in Resolute Bay. The voices, in many different accents, become a part of the daily

routine and we wait for them every evening — "Bathurst Island, Bathurst Island, how do you read," means it is Dave Gill's turn. "I read you five by five," means that Resolute Bay is coming through loud and clear. The voice at Resolute then replies, "I read you five by five also, go ahead please Dave," whereupon he relays the Bathurst Island weather. Occasionally he sets up schedules for longer broadcasts, depending on the group's needs. Stu, for example, sometimes talks to his two students on Seymour Island.

The nightly weather broadcast from all parts of the eastern high arctic usually takes the best part of an hour. Each field station takes its turn. It is, of course, also a good way to make sure that all is well with everyone in these remote regions.

Often the conversations are funny. Dave Gill tells the story of a man who had been working alone for some time. He regularly transmitted professional weather reports and appeared to be coping well with his lonely existence—until one night. When his turn came to transmit, he simply said, "The weather is lousy and there is nothing but ptarmigan shit everywhere." The man was taken out of the arctic that same day.

By 9 P.M. we are completely enclosed by fog. Nothing is visible past the camp ridge, the wind is still gusting up to thirty-five miles an hour, and the temperature is just above freezing. Rain keeps us all in camp.

◄ *King eider ducks*

More Wind and Rain

The weather has not improved. The wind is still blowing over the open expanses of Bathurst Island, but I set out anyway. Walking through Polar Bear Pass is a challenge. Wind gusts often slow my progress to a standstill. Ponds and pools of melt water have increased in size tenfold, and the rain, the sleet, and the strong wind continue to add more water to an already watery land. Small waves splash against lingering snowdrifts and turn them into ice hills.

King eider and old squaw ducks bustle about the pools of the great valley. A black-bellied plover's nest with three eggs lies momentarily deserted as I pass by. A parasitic jaeger flies above, searching for the nest, but is soon escorted out of the area by an aggressive plover.

A pair of sanderlings also appear to have established a nesting site in the valley. Both cross my path several times in the course of my walk through the soggy marsh. Obviously their nest is close by. One sanderling does his broken wing act trying desperately to attract my attention — chattering and waving back and forth, flopping from one extended wing to the other. I never do find the nest. There may be a good reason for not finding it, as sanderlings usually scrape a nest in higher, drier ground where vegetation is sparse or on some gravelly ridge or hilltop. Why, then, the broken wing act?

By noon the wind blows even harder and rain pelts against our parcoll. It is another good day for writing and drawing.

Stu's radio schedule with Seymour Island is the highlight of the day.

Seymour Island, an island of some three square miles just north of Bathurst Island, is inhabited by the only known ivory gull breeding colony in North America. For the past two years Stu, with the help of some students, has been studying the behaviour of these northern nomads. Last year Stu spent several months, with the help of one student, observing and documenting his findings. This year two students are further investigating the ivory gull.

Seymour Island and the surrounding polar pack ice is polar bear country. Seals are plentiful and attract many of the white bears. The students, two boys, have had problems earlier this season when a polar bear broke into a steel drum in search of food. The bear cut his paw during the burglary and became a nuisance around camp for some time. Polar bears are dangerous enough when healthy, let alone when hurt.

Over the radio we learn that all is well on Seymour.

Observing a Jaeger's Nest

After breakfast Mike McNall invites me to see his jaegers' nests. The walk takes us through parts of Polar Bear Pass, over the ridges south of camp, and past the Great Lake. One of the more impressive ridges we cross is Cemetery Ridge. Here, an assortment of rocks piled by nature stand like tombstones in a hauntingly lonely fashion overlooking the valley. It is an ideal place for snow bunting nests, and for weasels to hunt under the midnight sun.

In the valley we practically step on a plover's nest containing four large eggs. Irregularly speckled, they are either a golden or a black-bellied plover's eggs — we cannot agree which.

The marsh lands are in full swing. Creeks flow down the hillsides flooding the land below and leave little dry ground anywhere. Most creek bottoms are still ice covered. Water flows over these frozen creek beds creating yellow jagged lines through the otherwise dark marsh. Rain and a brief but heavy snowstorm remind us where we are, and the traditional Bathurst Island wind blows strong and cold, keeping us on the move.

Midway up a slope just west of the Great Lake and at its north end, Mike spots a long-tailed jaeger's nest. On the ground a shallow nest has been scraped. It contains one egg. On the many-textured ground and amid patches of partially blooming saxifrage, the small nest is hard to see, and it has taken Mike days of watching the adult birds to find it. One jaeger is sitting on the nest as we approach. It stays on the nest, nervously protecting its eggs until we get within twenty or thirty feet of it. Then it flies up and hovers directly above our heads threatening to attack.

Not wishing to upset the bird, we move on through the wetlands. At the extreme south end of the Great Lake, Mike has discovered the nesting site of a pair of parasitic jaegers, and he has been observing this particular pair for some time. Today, at last, he pinpoints their nest. I stay behind so as not to create too much of a disturbance. Upon Mike's approach the jaegers fly half a mile or so south of me, see me, and return to their original spot where Mike now sits.

The parasitic jaegers are larger and darker than their long-tailed cousins; their flight is even more impressive, and their general look is more streamlined.

On our way back, happy with our discoveries, we decide to stick to higher and drier ground. We cross over Cemetery Ridge. Here, under a flat slate-like stone, a snow bunting has built its nest. I have not seen many of these small birds—they have spread far apart and command large territories during their breeding season, but a few days ago I did see a single male perched on the bleached rib cage of a musk ox skeleton.

A pair of ruddy turnstones fly by, landing in front of us. They hang around on a hilltop looking suspicious.

Snow squalls, sleet, rain, and wind hurry us back to camp. Only a single golden plover perched on a lichen-covered rock appears not at all discomfited by the weather.

After dinner a herd of seven musk oxen appear on the hills directly across the Good Sir River. Only two miles away, they are feeding and making their way towards the far riverbank. It is fascinating to watch them through the scope. At times they are obscured by the low-hanging fog.

The Last Day on Bathurst

We awake to a calm and sunny day, but soon the clouds roll in, hail blows across the campsite, and the temperature drops.

A herd of musk oxen can be seen moving steadily towards camp. Often their dark silhouettes fade from sight when hidden by low-hanging fog. At each reappearance they are closer to the north bank of the Good Sir River.

Over the radio we are told that Stu and I are to be airlifted out of the camp at 9 P.M. today—if the weather is good. This seems unlikely as it continues to change drastically. From good to bad to worse and back again.

My last walk around the Bathurst camp takes me down to the eastern slope of the camp ridge to the bank of the Good Sir River. There I sit gazing across the Good Sir, watching the musk oxen feeding on the sparse vegetation. Slowly and deliberately the herd moves closer, oblivious of the camp, of the wind, and of the weather.

I walk upstream over the mud through partially formed creeks and over hummocks. In the opposite direction, by Eider Pond, the river is flowing freely. For a moment I cannot identify this new sound. Then I realize what has happened. The thaw is nearing completion and the sound of running water is becoming ever louder. Soon a major break in the ice barrier upstream of camp will fill the Good Sir with a great gush of water. But patches of wet snow will linger throughout the short summer. Bathurst Island is never completely snow free.

Three greater snow geese fly over Eider Pond towards Blow Out and fade into the landscape — a perfect finish for my last walk.

A short period of sunshine makes it possible for a twin Otter to land. Once again there is commotion on the tiny airstrip. Oil drums are shifted back and forth, full drums are unloaded, and empties are hoisted aboard. Our gear is soon aboard, too, and, by the time another hailstorm is ready to descend on the camp, we are on our way to Resolute.

The pilot, a man in his early fifties, ignores the weather. The hail and the bad visibility seem not to concern him. His confidence is transmitted to his passengers and we relax and enjoy the view.

Forty-five minutes later we land. Most of the snow that blanketed Resolute on my last visit has disappeared. There is mud everywhere instead.

The living quarters at the Polar Continental Shelf Project area are once again full. People are waiting to be airlifted to various places to carry out their summer projects. Little has changed since our last stay — only the faces are different.

We dine on lukewarm boiled potatoes and pork chops. But the ambience of the cookhouse is more relaxed than before — the head cook has gone south for his vacation.

Our accommodations are in a different spot this time. We get one of two six-by-ten-foot bedrooms in the back of the local entertainment centre. The entertainment centre consists of a pool table, a colour television with limited programming, a few chairs, a leatherette couch, and one oil stove. The raw plywood walls give it an un-finished, uninviting look.

This is to be our home for the next few days and there is really not much, except the decor, to complain about. We even have hot water. A large aluminum pot, occasionally topped up with snow, is heated constantly on top of the oil stove.

In the bedroom next to ours an archaeologist waiting for the rest of his working party to arrive is already snoring and there is little else to do but follow his example.

The sound effects and the dreary quarters make me homesick for the Bathurst camp. The image of Stu walking across Cemetery Ridge under the bright arctic sun a few days ago flits through my mind. His steady, deliberate walk and the expression of contentment on his gentle face revealed a great love and understanding for the barren land and embodied the peace that I found there.

From Resolute Bay we are to travel north to Penny Strait. Stu has arranged for us to be taken by helicopter to an area of Penny Strait which lies between the northern portion of Bathurst Island and the Grinnell Peninsula. He is to further investigate breeding populations of seabirds on some of the small islands in that most northern district, and I will tag along.

On to Penny Strait

We leave around 3:30 P.M. Tai Lo, our helicopter pilot and veteran of the Vietnam War, has charted a flight plan that will take us over the pack ice giving us a chance to observe animal activities on the way.

Our four-passenger helicopter flies straight north. The seat next to me in the rear is loaded with sleeping bags, extra fuel, food, and a rifle. We fly at an altitude of about forty-five hundred feet above the ice, which covers everything in every direction. Occasionally dark blue jagged lines break the monotony. The lines are cracks in the ice.

Along the cracks seals lie relaxing in the sun. From where we are, they look like children's toys. There are hundreds of ringed seals scattered along the few areas of open water. Here and there, expanded blow holes are also surrounded by seals. Most stay on the ice as we fly over them, but some disappear, plunging with lightning speed into the water of an ice crack. I think they are frightened more of our moving shadow than by the noise. Many of the larger seals' blow holes are submerged under green-blue melt water and form mini-lakes on the frozen white of the sea.

Farther north over the Queen's Channel, the ice has broken up, and the dark blue open sea, irregularly decorated with ice floes, is more interesting. Here, seabirds and walruses are enjoying their summer feeding grounds.

On one of the smaller ice floes two walruses sit looking bewildered by our noisy helicopter. The ice floe seems hardly large enough to bear the weight of their massive, shapeless bodies.

Overleaf: Snowy owl
Polar bear

A walrus will often grow to weigh sixteen hundred pounds or more and its movements on land are awkward. Like giant caterpillars, they pull themselves over a rocky island outcrop or over the uneven surface of an ice floe before plunging into the open sea. In the water they move with grace and speed, swimming and diving endlessly. Often large herds will line a beach of some isolated island, staying there for days without food, simply enjoying a spell of good weather.

Eskimos have hunted the walrus for centuries, but it was not until the white man started to hunt it that its survival as a species was endangered. A walrus makes an easy rifle target — it is fearless and huge.

This is polar bear country. Queen's Channel and Penny Strait are their hunting grounds. Here, seals are usually plentiful, supporting the roaming nomad bears on their summer journey north. Deep cobalt-blue paw impressions, freshly cast in the snow covering the ice, give us proof of their presence and before long we see our first bear. He is strolling aimlessly along the edge of the pack ice. His yellowish fur stands out against the white ice.

Tai flies lower, insisting that we have a closer look. Suddenly the bear gets excited — he starts to run around wildly and at full speed trying to get away from us. His nostrils are extended, his mouth open, and from constantly changing direction, he is soon exhausted and sprawls on the ice. Both Stu and I are embarrassed by the pilot's action. This is not the right way to observe polar bears in the wilds of the high arctic.

We have been in the air for more than an hour when Tai lands his helicopter on Sargent's Point on Bathurst Island. Days before, a single Otter has dropped off a fuel cache here. The helicopter, in a steady vertical descent, sits down within a foot of one of the oil drums and, with the aid of a manually operated hand pump, forty-five gallons of fuel are transferred from the drum to the aircraft.

Tai insists that the rifle, which he always carries with him in the helicopter in case of emergencies, be taken out of its case and made ready in case a polar bear should amble by. He is obviously greatly

◀   *Greater snow geese*

concerned with bear attacks, and I must admit one can hardly blame him. The stories told in the cookhouse at Resolute Bay of polar bears attacking humans are enough to strike fear in the bravest.

Last year two biologists from the Canadian Wildlife Service working in the eastern arctic were mauled by one. Both men were lucky to survive but apparently at one stage during the bear-man encounter the bear seized one of the researchers by the head and dragged him off to a more suitable feeding place. How the man finally broke loose and how the bear was shot, I don't know, but the men emerged the victors, and one of them has returned to the arctic this year — no doubt with much more respect for the great white bear.

We are off once again over the pack ice to Penny Strait. At Stu's request, Tai lands on a small flat island surrounded by open sea water. Here, hundreds of seabirds—common eiders, arctic terns, and different species of gulls—fly up and over both the open water and the ice in a frantic effort to avoid our helicopter. The island's shoreline is littered with common eider nests. Our helicopter has terrified the birds and the large, buff-coloured eider eggs lie bare and exposed to the cold air.

The eiders have covered some eggs with down before abandoning their nests. They, both male and female, are circling the tiny island waiting for us to leave.

Arctic terns have also nested here in shallow depressions in the gravelly ground. They are much more protective of their eggs than the eiders, not leaving their nests except to threaten to attack us.

We do not stay long. Another island farther north, surrounded by ice and open water, is to be our next stop. Our helicopter lands on the ice at the northernmost tip. The island barely protrudes out of the ice and snow. It is long and narrow and its terrain is more beautiful and more varied than the first island's. Gravel beaches, littered with common eider and arctic tern nests, surround three small freshwater melt ponds.

Lined with and surrounded by rusty red and olive green moss, the centre pond provides an excellent nesting site for a pair of red-throated loons. These, the most northerly distributed of all loons, swim nervously about the shallow water of the little pond. Time and time again one of the loons flies off, disappearing over the open sea. Its distant silhouette blends with the surrounding ice, water, and skyline. The loon's duck-like quacks identify it long before my eyes can identify its unique flying form.

Red-throated loons

The shallow melt pond contains no living aquatic animals; for this reason the adult loons must constantly fly to the open sea to feed themselves and their young. The nest, near the eastern shore of the pond, already contains two eggs. Usually no more than two eggs are laid per pair and often only one young is raised during each breeding season, with the result that the overall population of red-throated loons is always small.

Near a still smaller pond, at the south end of the island, Sabine's gulls act out some of their courtship behavior. These pigeon-sized, black-headed gulls have not yet prepared their nest, but will certainly do so within a few days.

Their courtship ceremony is serious and intense, leaving no doubt that this is to be their breeding ground. Their black heads and black

Polar bears near Penny Strait

wing tips contrast sharply with their otherwise white and blue-gray bodies and wing feathers, and give them the look of a rare, exotic species. The quick movements of their feet resemble a running shorebird's — not at all gull-like.

At the southernmost tip of the island, a flock of Brant geese are feeding, ignoring us completely. Arctic terns are everywhere. Often I can almost feel my hair being parted by a diving tern when I approach a nest too closely, and their shrill cries during these bombardments do not convince me that the whole exercise is merely a threat. (Our pilot drops to the ground or swings his hands and arms wildly when an arctic tern comes too close.)

We spend quite some time on this narrow strip of land, projecting so shallowly from the mostly frozen sea. Stu walks the island from end to end, examining nests and birds. He takes many photographs, and wants to return tomorrow to document and photograph more birds.

It is evening before we return to the helicopter. The sun is still shining, the arctic air is still chilly, and the wind still blows steadily across the open sea and ice. We are tired, cold, and hungry, and anxious to get back to Resolute. Tai heads the aircraft south towards Sargent's Point where we once again refuel from one of the drums. The rifle is rested on one of the fuel drums — but this time is not removed from its case.

Flying in a straight line towards Resolute Bay, Stu spots a flock of ivory gulls on the ice below. They are feeding on the remains of a seal that has recently been killed.

Tai sits the helicopter down on the ice, next to the seal. All that remains is the head of a seal and blood splattered over the ice. The still fresh bear tracks leading away from the feeding ground convince me that the best place to be is in the aircraft — among the many ice hummocks a polar bear can move freely without being detected by his victim.

Wildlife on Penny Strait

The next day we hope to hitch a ride to Ellesmere Island, but at 1:30 P.M. we are still hanging around the Polar Continental Shelf office building waiting for the latest weather report from Ellesmere. The weather at Resolute Bay is fine, but a snowfall on Ellesmere Island has made landing there dangerous.

One of the Bradley Air Service pilots has reported that several dead musk oxen have been sighted at Strathcona Fiord. Stu is anxious to examine them to find out why they died.

Time drags on and there is no improvement in the weather at Ellesmere Island, and it looks as though we will not get there. We have only a few days left before we have to return south to our jobs. I am bitterly disappointed; having heard so many glowing reports of the beauty of Ellesmere Island and its wildlife I am longing to see it.

Later in the afternoon, Stu, Tai Lo, and I are once again high over the frozen wastes heading back to the busy island in Penny Strait.

Our flight there takes us over land still waiting for the first spring thaw. Like a slumbering giant amoeba, blanketed by snow and ice waiting for the warmth of summer to revive it, the land mass below seems endless. The only thing moving is the shadow cast by our helicopter.

Three polar bears are strolling leisurely along the edge of a giant ice floe. A female bear and her two yearling cubs wander seemingly aimlessly, following the sharp line of blue and white separating the ice from the water. They appear oblivious of our noisy machine, not changing either pace or direction. Today their yellowish fur coats are highlighted by the sunshine and stand out against the blue ice hummocks.

Another stop at Sargent's Point to take on more fuel is necessary. Refueling is becoming more work each time we land here. The fuel cache of four oil drums has been dropped haphazardly. One drum has landed standing on end while the other three lie about on their sides on the thawing ground. Of course we deprived the upright drum of its contents first. Then the drum lying closest to the flattest piece of ground was emptied, where the helicopter could sit most horizontally. Now, the third drum to be decanted has to be rolled up a slight incline, then stood up on its end. We manage it all without complications, and it warms us on this windy, chilly day.

The flight from Resolute via Sargent's Point to the shallow island in Penny Strait takes approximately one and a half hours. The helicopter lands on the pebble beach on the east side of the island. The engine is turned off and only the sounds of the island's inhabitants can be heard.

Most of the birds ignore us and go about their business.

Arctic terns are busily flying back and forth from the island to the open water looking for food. Red phalaropes swim about the centre pond. Only the red-throated loons bob about the melt pond observing our every move. At the extreme southern end, the Brant geese are still wandering about calmly.

Today Stu is better equipped to take photographs—he has brought huge telephoto lenses.

We each set out in a different direction so as not to interfere with one another. Tai carries his rifle in a leather strap over his shoulder.

Fresh bear tracks are pressed into the island mud. Yesterday there were many common eider nests; today there are none. The bear has walked around the whole perimeter of the island and has destroyed and eaten all the eider eggs. We cannot find one nest intact, nor one egg. Mangled egg shells and polar bear tracks are all that remain.

We spend several hours on the island. The place is as active as a beehive. Birds come and go and arctic terns vocalize an angry tune at any approach of their nests. I sit for long stretches of time on different parts of the island observing and photographing species I might not see again for some time — red-throated loons, Sabine's gulls, Brant geese, common eider ducks.

Stu and I want to stay, but Tai has heard over the helicopter radio that bad weather is rapidly approaching the Resolute area. He is anxious to return to home base.

An ivory gull in flight

The flight back takes a lot longer. Strong winds slow our speed to a snail's pace. Tai is becoming more and more concerned about getting back to Resolute in time, and after we have landed safely I understand his concern. Within an hour, the wind begins to howl around the wooden buildings and another snowstorm envelops Resolute Bay.

A Summer Storm

The fifty-mile-per-hour winds persist, driving heavy snow across the town. Many of the exposed outside walls of the low buildings are plastered with a thick crust of snow. All planes are secured to withstand the storm, but even so, one is blown into an aircraft hangar wall causing damage to both plane and hangar.

Nothing is moving anywhere. People sit around the cookhouse, and meals are the highlight of this wintry July day.

Towards evening the storm subsides. By midnight the sun is again shining brightly and the several inches of snow that have fallen are melting.

The weather forecast is excellent! We are to get one more chance to fly to Ellesmere Island on the following day.

The Last Day: The First Wolf

The weather is good. The sun is out and even the wind is relatively subdued. Most important of all, we are flying in the familiar single Otter airplane in a northerly direction towards Ellesmere Island.

The objective of this excursion is for Mel Veau to fly to Strathcona Fiord on Ellesmere to transport a group of people from one research site to another. At Eureka, north of Strathcona Fiord, our single Otter is to be refueled at the Bradley Air Service Camp and we are to return to Resolute late today.

An hour after leaving Resolute we encounter dense fog. Soon, we are totally engulfed. By the time our single Otter climbs above the fog and cloud cover, the weather has once again improved and only an occasional thin white cloud drifts by the windows. Below are great expanses of frozen sea and partially snow-covered land masses. The land projecting from the sea ice becomes more and more uneven. Gentle slopes gradually turn into rounded, snow-free hilltops surrounded by unevenly sculptured ice.

Our cabin area is crowded. Oil drums, large wooden crates, sleeping bags are everywhere. I am sitting next to several full forty-five gallon oil drums. They are strapped together and fastened to the inner framework of the plane. Landings here are often bumpy and everything is always carefully packed and fastened. I, too, am strapped in tightly in the tiny canvas seat. The aircraft cabin is cold.

Two hours later Mel discovers a snow-free strip of beach below. He loses altitude to inspect this landmark at closer range. Circling the strip several times he decides to test the firmness of the exposed ground. The test run is accomplished by rolling the Otter aircraft on its two main body wheels over the beach. Half way across Mel revs up the engine, we pick up speed and are airborne again. We circle the beach once more. The impressions made by the aircraft wheels are shallow, proving that the ground is solid enough to land on. We approach again and land smoothly, close to the end of the strip.

I have no idea why we have landed here and cannot ask because of the noise. Not until the aircraft has come to a full stop do I realize why. Two oil drums are pushed out of the loading door, falling three feet to the ground, and leaving impressions deeper than those made by the wheels. We roll the drums to one side of the runway so that they will not interfere with takeoff. Mel taxies to the far end of the beach and uses me as a marker at the other end to judge distance.

Mel waves to me, indicating that he has it all figured out. The distance between me and the airplane does not seem to be all that great, yet the engine sounds muffled and distant—the wind blowing through ice hummocks and the sound of my boots crunching and sliding over the gravelly beach are much louder than the roar of the plane. Fresh polar bear tracks are the only sign that another living thing has passed this way. Several old squaw ducks fly low and silently among the hummocks.

I felt desolation on Bathurst Island, but, for a single moment standing alone on that lonely beach, I realize the full meaning of the word. Here is wilderness in its untampered state.

Our takeoff is as smooth as our landing and we are off over the frozen sea. The farther north we go, the more open water. I have been told that on Ellesmere spring is usually well advanced compared to other high arctic islands. This proves to be so, and the more I see of Ellesmere, the more inviting it looks. The uneven, mountainous terrain below reminds me of a three-dimensional school map in a deserted classroom. Fiords carved into land masses make me think of Vikings.

We have to fly to Eureka as Strathcona Fiord is fogged in. All our destinations are only places — often there are no permanent buildings. In fact, rarely are there man-made structures of any kind.

For some time Mel follows the rugged outline of Ellesmere Island where the open sea separates land from pack ice. The weather continues to be good. From our vantage point we look down on sunshine highlighting mountain tops, cloud patches, sea ice, and cliffs that disappear into the blue water of the fiords.

The landscape gradually changes from mountains to desert, and eroded sandstone projects high over the tundra floor. Somewhere below a pair of gyrfalcons have nested for years, raising its broods in an ancient nest piled high with the bones of arctic hares.

Some years ago Stu photographed and observed the gyrs. We fly over the nest, straining to see some signs of life. But we see only the deserted nest, whitewash still marking the edge.

The landing facilities at Eureka are excellent. A well-cared for runway, long enough for transport planes to land on, and with complete refueling facilities nearby, are Eureka's dominant features. I have pictured another Resolute, but a few plywood shacks at one end of the runway and one more permanent-looking two-storey building are all there is. Some of the makeshift houses are still identifiable by crudely painted signs over their doorways. One says "Canadian Wildlife Service," others have abbreviations of some university or museum whose researchers have worked in the area. This year no one is working here.

The mountainous countryside, accented with patches of fresh snow, makes Eureka the most beautiful place I have seen in the high arctic. I am told that arctic wolves often prowl the camp under the midnight sun.

While eating a leisurely lunch in the Bradley Air Service main building, Mel keeps in radio contact with the field party at Strathcona Fiord. It seems that the fog is disappearing and within a short time we will be able to land there.

Our plane, refueled, is once again airborne, heading for a valley in the Strathcona Fiord area.

We fly over an arctic hare colony a few miles from the Eureka camp. This is one of the largest known arctic hare colonies in the high arctic. Unfortunately, we have to fly at a high altitude to avoid the mountain tops so we do not see them. On Bathurst Island where arctic hares are less numerous and are difficult to find, I saw only their skeletons. But several hares did raise their young near the Bathurst Island camp

Arctic hare ▶   *Overleaf: Red phalarope*
                                                                    Weasel

BUERSCHAPER '76

BUERSCHAPER '76

down by the Good Sir River some years before. And each day one female would swim across the river to feed on the other side, returning to her young when she had finished.

We fly over snow-covered mountains and great valleys. The land is sculptured in a seemingly endless variety of shapes and forms. In one of the valleys we see what first appear to be moving dots on the valley floor. They turn out to be human figures huddling around some crates and oil drums — waiting for us. This is the field party from the Carnegie Museum that is to be transported to another valley nearby.

Our plane frightens a herd of musk oxen that have been grazing on the slopes close to the valley's edge. They disappear behind a hilltop.

Mel circles the plane several times before deciding on a landing site. He chooses a strip of gravelly ground in the centre of the valley and after landing we taxi to the waiting field party.

◀ *Arctic wolf*

The Carnegie Museum people have been camping here for several weeks. They tell us of six musk oxen that lie dead scattered throughout the valley. And that morning they have seen a white arctic wolf who visited their camp in search of food, then vanished in the hills.

The gear of the Carnegie Museum researchers is loaded on the airplane. Our sleeping bags are unloaded and one rifle is left at our disposal. The plane takes off.

Stu and I set out in the general direction of where a dead musk ox has been seen. Carrying the rifle still in its case on my right shoulder, we walk steadily over the muddy ground. In front of us, still some distance away, a dark silhouette rises from the ground like a large boulder. It is the woolly remains of a musk ox. A short distance to the left another carcass breaks the flatness of the valley floor.

Stu wants to remove from each dead beast a leg bone, later to study its marrow consistency, and to collect the lower jaw to be used to determine the animal's age. Our walk is interrupted by the discovery of several mummified bodies of greater snow geese. They are completely dehydrated and extremely well preserved. In the arctic decay is slow. The cause of their death is an enigma. They have not been killed by a predator, as their bodies are intact.

The valley is eerie. Why is this beautiful spot, surrounded by rolling hills and snow-covered mountain tops, littered with the bodies of its inhabitants? Has the previous winter been so harsh?

But we have already seen a herd of healthy musk oxen, and ringed plovers fly low just ahead of us. And in the mud are tracks—wolf and arctic fox. Some are a fair-sized arctic wolf's—probably a male's. They appear to be only a few hours old. Other tracks are smaller and older, probably a female's.

The musk ox has been dead for some time. Its eyes have sunk into its skull, its woolly body smells of decay, and flies have deposited millions of eggs on its matted fur. The thought of cutting into the stale flesh is repellent. Stu, however, is determined, and proceeds to carve away the hind leg. I am of little help. All I can do is steady the hindquarter and help separate the thick fur so that Stu can find the junction where the leg joins the hip.

The operation goes quite well. The patient is dead in any case, so what can go wrong? The leg bone is removed and deposited in a plastic garbage bag and tightly sealed—not only to trap the bone but also the aroma.

The next step is to remove the lower jaw. The procedure is the same. I stand and watch, occasionally grabbing a handful of fur away from where Stu is carving. The stench of decaying flesh becomes stronger and stronger the further the operation progresses. Thank God for the ever-present arctic wind that blows fresh air over our operating table! Finally the lower jaw, severed from the head, is securely wrapped in another garbage bag.

At least six musk oxen have died mysteriously and lie scattered throughout the valley. Only two are within our reach. By the time we get to our second musk ox, I am almost glad that we have only time enough to work on two of the dead beasts. The smell of decay hangs heavily over the remains, and another million flies have worked on this one, making our job even more dismal. Even Stu hesitates, and circles the animal several times before deciding that we should turn the body on to its other side before dissecting the leg and jaw.

This side is still frozen to the ground. It is difficult to turn it over. Each of us grabs a leg. My leg suddenly snaps — sending me flying over the body and coming to rest on the other side desperately trying to control my balance.

It is not the neatest way to remove a leg bone but it will do. The stench becomes overwhelming and a prompt decision is made not to remove this beast's jaw.

We cannot tell why these two musk oxen have died. They do not appear to be old. Both have massive bruises on their hindquarters and the marrow of the broken bone is pink. (The bone marrow of a well-nourished musk ox is yellow, indicating a high fat content.) Did they die of starvation or from injuries received in a battle among themselves?

The valley is silent. Only the ringed plovers that occasionally cross our path disturb the quiet with their calls. In the distance, where the "Expedition Fiord" camp stood, only a single oil drum remains.

We have accomplished what we set out to do, so we head back towards the lone oil drum where Mel is to pick us up. In a stretch of sparsely grass-covered ground, several shorebird chicks run in all directions trying hard to avoid us. These are the young of the ringed plovers that vociferously object to our intrusion as we cross their territory.

Halfway back to the campsite our single Otter appears over the hilltops, lands, and stops by the oil drum. Mel has completed his mission and we must leave "Death Valley." If ever I wish for fog, it is now. It would be fascinating to be stranded here for a day or two.

No such luck. The remaining forty-five gallons of fuel are quickly pumped into the fuel tank, the empty drum is loaded aboard, the doors are closed tight, the engine starts, and we are ready for takeoff.

Suddenly, Stu or Mel — I don't know exactly who — spots something moving. "A wolf" is all I hear over the roar of the airplane engine before I unfasten my seatbelt, lunge for the cargo door, whip it open, and jump to the ground. I run towards the white figure that is moving steadily towards me.

Mel has shut off the engine and follows with rifle and camera. The wolf keeps coming. Within twenty or thirty feet of me he stops and stares. I kneel, hoping not to frighten him away. He closes the distance between us by a few more hesitant steps; then, in a semi-circle, walks around me. His nostrils expand and contract and he does not take his eyes off me. For a moment I am unsure of his intentions. But he sniffs the ground and trots off, disappearing in the rolling hills.

We reboard, taxi to a stretch of firm ground, and fly out over the most picturesque country I have ever seen. Low-hanging clouds, snow-covered mountain tops, great valleys, endless frozen deserts of pack ice amid seemingly barren arctic islands.

We land in Resolute about 9 P.M. The sun is bright but the Polar Continental Shelf Project buildings are quiet. All the arctic researchers have left for their respective outposts. Others have gone south to celebrate the weekend.

Stu and I have just enough time to pack our gear, wash off the Ellesmere Island mud, and head for the airport to fly home.